THE BIRD HOVERER

by Aaron Belz

BlazeVOX [books]

Buffalo, New York

The Bird Hoverer by Aaron Belz

ISBN: 1-934289-27-2   ISBN 13: 978-1-934289-27-3
Library of Congress Control Number: 2006938681

BlazeVOX [books]
14 Tremaine Ave
Kenmore, NY 14217

Editor@blazevox.org

publisher of weird little books

BlazeVOX [books]

blazevox.org

2   4   6   8   0   9   7   5   3   1

Acknowledgments

Poems in this volume have appeared in the following publications:

Canary: "Clare Considers," "Peasants in the Woods"
Can We Have Our Ball Back: "The Mystery I Wrote," "O Sisters," "Observations and Recommendations"
Curiobox: "Bells," "The End of My Computer," "The End of My Computer," "For Walt Whitman," "The Topographical Air Assault"
Delmar: "The Berbers"
Drunken Boat: "Canaries"
Elimae: "The Bungee Cord Experiment," "The Man with No Hat," "Marxism"
Exquisite Corpse: "A Horseshoe of Roses"
Fine Madness: "Map Tools"
Jacket: "In Bed with Meryl Streep," "Tim Burton Explodes"
The Hat: "Nicely," "Pushkin"
Kulture Vulture: "Two Criminals"
LIT: "2005 Is an Important Year for Alec Baldwin"
Matter: "Things That Tend Not to Collapse"
McSweeney's: "Pam"
Mudfish: "The Preserve"
The New Pantagruel: "Leaf"
No Tell Motel: "My Factotum," "My Factotum," "My Factotum"
Pierogi Press: "Seven Bastions"
Raised in a Barn: "Two Sides of a Story"
RealPoetik: "Smartest Creatures"
Unpleasant Events Schedule: "Fifteen Poems that End with 'Good Luck'"

Some of these poems were also included in a chapbook entitled
Plausible Worlds (Observable Books, 2005).

I. Among Birds

THE PRESERVE

I'm on a lone bench in the dark.

Owls strain their eyes, and I feel their look,
and the chain at the park
gate clanks shut.

The apparitions of children with neon
frisbees rotate around the barbecue—
here come aunts with slippery bathing suits,
and the wiffle father, the dark shepherd.

           A car engine
mulling through this public wood could
be the ranger's, whose headlights
flush up the ground-nesting birds
till they scatter like spiders in the sky.

Behind the treeforms the moon hangs strange,
mooing, bowing like a butler—
everything in the park is unwanted—

a sea of woodpeckers rises to the fore.

Like a dish or a shirt now I lay me down
on the bench as a fawn paws surreally past,
and I cuddle my nylon jacket to me in the chill.

SMARTEST CREATURES

Birds should be quiet.
Birds should pray.

Dolphins have no idea what they're talking about.
Dolphins don't sleep.

Birds run their fingers through their hair as they talk.
Birds run into windows.

Dolphins ought to shut up.
Dolphins are smooth like bottles.

Birds underappreciate sympathy.
Birds would love to go swimming with you on Sunday.

Dolphins feel pain as they think about the past.
Dolphins go everywhere naked.

Birds assume they own the world.
Birds, in fact, are middle class.

Dolphins win you over with unexpected comments.
Dolphins strive for peace.

Birds consume whatever people give them.
Birds die dissatisfied.

LEAF

It is not sad, this invented leaf,
Because it does bend in the wind
The way daisies do in a sweet shower,
Because it stains, as it breaks under
the pressure of my thumb, my thumb;
Or rather it is invisibly sad,
Because it is invisible to the eye
And no more an invention than a word,
This *leaf*, here forever, the last email
Sent by one who swore *never again*,
Once in the inbox, now deleted,
A whole branch full of words
That had grown, if not out of love
Or sweet, false, virtuous showers,
Out of each of our desperation to know
And to be known by one another.

CANARIES

The jackknife you filched
with etchings of boxing gloves on it
reminded me of the metal fruit
in the center of the table at Canaries Street,

for both were perfectly round
and gave off an inaudible hum
like that of a remote dishwasher.
When Susan came bounding down the stairs

with her arms full of teen magazines
and hollered something to Rudy
about your new jackknife,
I came in from the field where

I had been sitting in a lather
about my cracked telescope case.
I said, *Rudy's not in earshot, sister,*
he ran out for decorative pomegranates;

the Lipscombs are coming tonight
and we want the place fresh and ready.
And I saw you skinning yams
over a mixing bowl in the kitchen.

Not with your inexplicably spherical penknife,
but with a small, tangled fork
of only two tines, in our factorylike
residence on Canaries Street.

RAVENS AT THE ZOO

A flock of ravens followed me to the zoo:
there, they pecked at my soda.

I looked up, and they pecked at my eyes.
They sat upon my shoulders and relieved themselves.

I am almost too modest to relate these details.
White spots began appearing on my shoes.

My hat felt too tight, so did my glasses.
So did my pants, even though they were new.

Something about these birds was causing me to grow.
I expanded, slowly, for the better part of the afternoon.

What was it about the ravens that prompted
what might best be termed an odd physiological reaction?

CLARE CONSIDERS

Clare considers the sane and insane patterns of the mind.
What carved them there she will never know.
All she can do is look at hippopotamuses now,
while the brochure in her hand rustles in the wind.

We love to talk about Jesus and forgiveness at the zoo
among antelope, snakes, and bears that should not be there.
Though feelings coil confusedly, the parrots are clear,
perhaps bright denizens of where we ourselves should go.

Water-dwelling animals control their slippery humps
as Clare and I suck on cones of crushed and flavored ice.
I think about the fact that we are the same in many ways,
yet different in profounder ones. I walk with a limp,

she without. I drive a van, Clare a white Accord.
In both our pockets jingle pennies pressed with our names,
our shoes are hot against the asphalt. We are the same,
yet different. I own a house she could never afford.

She is still in high-school yet seems, in some ways, old.
She comments on the wonderful texture of elephant ears.
We both struggle against darkness, but against different fears.
We are a grizzly and a cub, a glue-horse and a foal.

AMONG BIRDS

Having spent the better part of the morning
among birds, having heard
                              what they whisper
to each other as the sun comes up,

having noted how they name their offspring,
with names like Fuzz Packet and Mr. Charming,
Devily Doo and The Potato Famine Boy,

having observed, if momentarily,
as they begin to glide, their haughty eyes
and knife-like toes,
                         I hereby reject birds
                         and not only birds but
the places where they dwell, the patterns
of their lives, the very cosmic instinct
that brings them into being—in fact, the skies;

having been raised by birds and
having nursed at their impossible teats
and been subjected to their whimsical
sarcasm, also having been approached by
them on several occasions—

when my star had risen and theirs perhaps had not—

                         in the name of
neighborliness or good citizenship and having
politely asked them to step off,
                       can't you see
I'm busy, type of thing, and having quietly
informed them that I no longer belong
to their so-called tribe,

                              I hereby request
that they wipe the silly smirks off their faces
and find other people to circle, other places
to drop their glob-like feces, and that is all
I ask of them, not that we can't exist on the same
planet, free-thinking individuals,
                                        in equal

if separate and clearly demarcated communities.

ANDREA AND THE BEES

A yellow fusion of gradients,
These bees whirled up *en masse*

And away from Andrea's storm gutter
While she banged

A shovel on the siding.
The insects growled off into the wind

And a new hurricane rose
Up, a violent thing from Spain

Carrying obsolete artifacts, chimney
Bricks, tar paper. Andrea

Ran into her house bleating,
Crying out for mercy.

Then seven stacks of blue lightning
Pinioned the seven corners of the earth

Throwing huge volts
Among the dying trees of Andrea's

Neighborhood, making the night day.
She got out her power binoculars

And peered from her bay window, and she saw
It was her religion coming to get her.

MARXISM

Let me ask you something, Shonda.
How did you get so good on organ?

*I practiced a lot when we lived in Oregon.
I mainly played a lilting rondo.*

So let me ask you something else;
would you join me for wine and sturgeon?

*I'll join you if we don't use knives.
My other husband was a surgeon.*

I understand. One of my wives
trafficked cocaine in money belts,

and I never wore one thereafter.
I know it's a little bit different.

*Well, whatever pays the rent
is what I say. In the hereafter*

*such things won't matter, Bill, will they?
Let's bladeless dine on fish and wine.*

In heaven it will all be fine.
Here we still practice chivalry.

MAP TOOLS

A voice announced, *The crematorium is closing now.*
Please, everyone, proceed to the new infirmary.

So I did, and *voilà*—my liver spots were cured!
Now I have to figure out what to do with

all these El Producto boxes of map tools
my grandfather left me, from his vast estate.

Pilot Bill may want them, the poor old cluck;
restoring a steamboat must challenge the nostrils.

That's what he was doing before Viv cried,
Pass me a Mergenthaler, I'm going down.

The sea is really green over here. Bill?
Then she became one with something dark,

and I was finishing the lighting of the lamps,
so I could just barely see her from here.

You see, I had burned a notch out of my nail
with the torch, so the air smelled like lemons,

and my heart felt all bombed out, the way it does
when someone you vaguely know dies suddenly,

and you wonder what must keep the stars on their spindles,
or what keeps the tickers clacking in rows along the street.

PEASANTS IN THE WOODS

Mary begins her assignment.
It is to write a creative essay called
"Peasants in the Woods."
Who assigned this?

The first sentence of her first draft is,
"Once there were peasants wandering the woods."
No good, she thinks. But continues.
"These were kindly peasants."

Mary crumples it up and begins afresh.
"Peasants, peasants. Why the funny hats?
Why the long faces?"

Mary crumples it up and begins afresh.
"I am not Mary. This is not my assignment.
I am Aaron Belz. I am a poet."

What is wrong with the person who assigned this?
Who is this person? What does he/she want from me?
Mary thinks.

Soon, her sister shows up, and they leave
for the mall. It's sunny outside the mall.
The mall itself turns out to be full of peasants.
"Peasants in the Mall." By Mary.
She thinks.

THE MYSTERY I WROTE

The mystery I wrote calls the reader's attention to four things:
> a smoking chimney,
> a field,
> a sleeping animal,
> and a desperate woman.

The chimney looks about as you'd expect.
The field might be a bit yellower and more barren
than you'd imagine.
The animal could be a skunk.
The woman is pulling her shirt off as she runs, uttering short,
> sharp shrieks.

It's on fire! Her shirt is burning!
Now, this is not a full-fledged mystery; it's sort of a tall tale.
And truth be told, the woman is a man; but you don't know that at
first.
"She" runs *away from* a house, *past* a sleeping skunk, and
> *through* a field...

But you see, you *assumed* there was a house—and there was,
> what with the chimney.

The smoke is the giveaway, though.
The smoke and the skunk.

ARIZONA BEACH

I saw something interesting at Arizona Beach.
It was a man with three golf balls in his mouth.
He stood in such a way that the people around him laughed.
He was darting his eyes back and forth like a prostitute.
He also had a large stick of chalk in his hand.
He was spelling something in the air.
I could read it, and I'll tell you what it said:
Go away, you vast band of gypsies.
Leave me to my boom box and surf board.
I've almost had it with this two-horse town.
This man could not have been a lunatic.
He was too dexterous, and besides he was wearing a suit.

Off to the right of this scene there was a bonfire.
On the bonfire people were baking fresh clams.
I'll tell you something, these people were the salt of the earth.
Some of them were playing air guitars and humming.
One of the women wore a red neckerchief.

When I left for more hoagies the sun was declining.
The day was waning, the dusk was waxing.
I really stubbed my toe on a sand-covered board.
Then, almost inaudibly, a sound made itself heard.
It was the sound of thousands of ants crying out for peace.
It was the thin chant of marchers descending on a capitol.
There were voices of prisoners requesting release
and the small sound of chomping, as of children eating apples.

I saw some interesting things at Arizona Beach.
Among them, a man with three golf balls in his mouth.

WHEREVER I GO

Wherever I go
there are two of you:
one telling me what to do,
the other what not to do.

I'm going to stab you with a fork.

COUNTRY TRIPTYCH

Scarecrow

Scarecrow, scarecrow, what have you heard?
I've heard about the blackbird and nothing more.
What of the moon, shining bright on this night?
I haven't heard of that. Like I said, just the blackbird.

Blackbird

Blackbird, good friend, what do you know?
I know of the scarecrow and nothing else.
What of the corn in its thousands of rows?
Dude, just the scarecrow. Are you deaf?

Conclusio

The scarecrow was marginally nicer than the blackbird.
Both were somewhat flippant, but the blackbird
was really kind of a jerkoff. He needs treatment.
They both need treatment, but the blackbird needs it more.

THE BUNGEE CORD EXPERIMENT

We have failed with the bungee cord experiment.
We have disgraced ourselves in front of our friends.
Yesterday all was cake-making and merriment;
today our funding inevitably will come to an end.

If you think back to the whole scooter debacle,
you might see that it was the beginning of a trend.
We knew the feather-cushion seat would tickle.
We could have guessed the rubber kickstand would bend.

Years ago, in college, we had our heads screwed on.
We carried notebooks everywhere we went
and asked questions of the freshmen on the lawn.
Even in grad school we said what we meant:

A blue car travels northeast at 18 miles per hour.
A red truck travels the same direction at the same speed.
How long before each driver needs a shower?
Our approach was pure science, rigorous indeed.

But slowly, over time, things seemed to degenerate.
Things fell apart, if you'll permit me that cliché.
What once was instantaneous now produced a wait.
We found ourselves going out at night to make hay.

And now, after fifteen years of work and trying,
the sum of all our thought has gone awry.
But there's no progress made in hopeless sighing.
We'll rethink the bungees. And they'll work, by and by.

PAM

For a laxative, try eating a little Pepsodent.
None of us enjoy that more than Pam,
Who once worked at a toothpaste factory.
Pam is now president of Berkman Lumber
And could kick your ass at the drop of a hat.
She no longer needs a laxative as powerful as that.

She has developed these huge muscles that
Enable her to pop a closed tube of Pepsodent
Simply by placing it under her hat,
Smiling, and saying, *My name is Pam,*
I supervise the workers at Berkman Lumber,
Though I used to work at a toothpaste factory.

Pam sometimes wanders back to that factory
Transfixed by the fumes of an industry that
She grew up with. The aroma of lumber
Soon beckons her back, her Pepsodent
Smile reassuring the workers who chant, *Pam!*
Pam! Pam! as she takes off her hat.

Because of her, each of them has a hat
Too, but not like the hats back at the factory,
Which are white and sterile; they are like Pam's,
Tall and shiny and multicolored, with a logo that
Says, instead of *Welcome to Pepsodent,*
EVERYONE LOVES YOU AT BERKMAN LUMBER.

Sometimes the hats tip or fall off, bumped by lumber
Or a ladder. Pam insists that everyone needs a hat
Just like we had back at Pepsodent.
She basically wants to run the mill like a factory
Even though the Berkman board has told her that
The world does not revolve around Pam.

The board can bite me, scoffs Pam,
I am the president of Berkman Lumber,
The foreman, the head. This is the house that
Pam built! Workers cheer, throw their hats
In the air, like folks do back at the factory—
They roar as Pam pops a tube of Pepsodent

By saying a few words as she places it under her hat.
But inside, she is remembering the factory,
Whispering to herself, *Welcome to Pepsodent.*

NICELY

The grainy ice lies nicely, nicely,
the stinking crocuses in the glen
provoke hummingbirds to feistiness,
and me and my aunts bat piñatas, piñatas.

THE VELVET SPIKES

One machine had a broken language button.

As if to mute the first two clanks,
none of the cars were visible at the university,
and I could still taste cereal
beneath the obligatory horse jelly.

Old wolverines and marines make great referees.

Along about the first open section, two of our fastest mates
made a break for the middle and then at the same time
sped up and split apart laterally.

Time for a quick chestnut, time for a nap.
A video reel pulls noisily through its rotors,
though we finished the feature five minutes ago.
A thudding of bolts: you with your free silencer,

me with my photos of Italy, weeping.

THAT PEN

Without the ostentation of the upper-gard,
novice chair-thrower asks for a salute.
I fed it to milky, the bird hoverer replies,
nodding at Axwhite and his Alice painting.

I spotted her in Kile, says the old grammarian.
That vision had grated on our horse carbuncle
so splinteringly as to kale off any glee.
I spotted her with the maitre d', says Kor.

How prosaic of you, banal proselyte in
my terrace, frog-leaping concugard.
Dirt that pen, you hopper slash chanter,
without the ostentation of the upper-gard.

Here again is novice chair-thrower, head
painted ochre, slobber on his beak,
and I ask him for a moment of heart
ankle. Something like that to write with.

I allayed Maxy's sanitation lettuce chopper
and remedied the ex-Spanish Trotskyite's
monkey dong, with only a padded flick,
with a chip of tang at my bald magnet,

said mirrored Merwin, silt-besmirched.

FIFTEEN POEMS THAT END WITH "GOOD LUCK"

Old Titan

Misty owned a nanny named Old Titan.
She used to milk her for cheese,
But when slaughtering day came
Oh boy, Tony Graffanino!
Good luck.

Mickelthwaite

The home of the undressed crabapple tree,
Onesacre claims among its distinguished former residents
An acne-pocked man by the name of
Good luck.

Susan, Glimpsed

In the parking lot of extinguished ambition
Comes now one John Mickelthwaite,
Above-average clairvoyant
Just getting out of a Nissan Sentra.
Good luck.

Tuxedo Sunset

I live for these goblets of booze
And the aptly-named Jenni who brings them
Two at a time, along a path among pines,
As if one camera weren't enough:
Good luck.

The Parade

What the milkman drinks.
What the postman reads.
What the Indian buys.
Good luck.

A Cracked Pansy

Flattened into its hairy haunches,
A cracked pansy lay teething among turnips
On rotted hinds fresh from the kills
That burble behind the trees that line Van Vliet Street.
Good luck.

A Certain Killjoy

O vending machine man,
Stop whistling that pedantic macramé of filth,
Clamoring over trunks stamped
Absolutely awesome.
My name is Hofstra.
Good luck.

Jammin'

Skip the Shedd's Spread, monsignor:
This frappe calls for vegemite,
Or my name's not Krull.
Potato. Potato!
The wheel is busted, so
Good luck.

Country Things

The mind bends anymore
At even the mention
Of Iowa, its long sheds,
Careful tracks among lambs.
Good luck.

Aptitude

I was opened, flipped and then
Desired the company of a stooge.
Do not be surprised if this happens to you,
Mr. Aptitude Barnaby Filament Drood.
Good luck.

A Can of Plates

You love the girl; the girl loves you.
And then you find in a spoonful of stew
A circus peanut, a tree, and a screw:
Something evil is happening to you.
Good luck.

Uzbekistan

Your Mini wends its way through Tajikistan.
Children slap fresh clips in Kalashnikovs.
Suddenly you wish you were skiing in Pakistan.
Good luck.

Uncle Fuddly

They called my grandpa Uncle Fuddly
Before, during, and after
His death by prostate cancer.
Yuck!
Good luck.

Faneuil Hall

I met a girl at Faneuil Hall
Named Fanny L. Hill.
Isn't that bizarre?
Isn't it a bazaar?
Good luck.

These United States

Dear President Bukkake,
I'm stranded in Wichita
Because my beaver broke down.
Please send the Elias Sports Bureau.
Dear Mr. Belz,
Good luck.

BELLS

Man. What a day.
I woke up with a jellied crab
clinging to my bone.
My coffee tasted like
poultice. Under the newspaper
was a white malice shaped
like Daphne du Maurier,
except it had no spoon
to tease out its bonnet,
and so it stayed very still.
It sort of slept there.
Unwilling to look at the sun
I buttered my doughnut
as usual, then put on my
12-string and ambled out
for more ends. The only sad
thing left was a Chevy,
stooped in its own sandwich.
I rubbed my eyes, wiped
a gigabyte on my shirttail,
then looked again:
This time it rose powerful,
though still sad, much
like a wave blending buffoons.
I love you, I muttered,
as if to myself. *I love you
too*, I muttered back.

APES

38

I love the decentralized subway system.
It goes from California to Laos.
In California, there are connected windows.
In Laos you lose those, but they do have apes.

STELLA

A woman, eating nothing but Viet Nam,
sat in the shadow of a bushel of parsnip.
She beckoned me to explode daily.
Upon closer inspection, she graphed
moon events without any sort of lake
effect. I said, *That's what's called
the "lake effect."* She said, *I bought
these balls in Bali on sale.* She winced.
I cleaned my watch. We urged the stars.

THE TOPOGRAPHICAL AIR ASSAULT

During the topographical air assault,
I slept on the wind porch with Martha.
I mean, we slept in the same place,
not together. It was a trick-move
people learn who have been alive
for awhile. A reverse arm collapse.
A matriarchal half-spin, with coffee.
During the air assault, as I was saying,
Martha and I each ate a magazine
coated in hornet guts. Once inside
the imaginary meat tunnel, we smiled.
We knew the assault was almost over,
and that we'd made it through scathed
only by our own predilections
as in the background an electric guitar
strummed unfamiliar arpeggios.
Mine was *Men's Life*, by the way.

II. Names of the Lost

TWO SIDES OF A STORY

i.

Hello, my name is Thomas Johnston.
I have made myself into a chess expert
by spending two weeks in Bali
with world-renowned chess champion
Anatoly Karpov. Simply by watching
Anatoly's moves I have been able
to intuit chess principles that are older
than you and I put together—older
even than Kasparov, Kramnik, and Spassky
and their wives put together. The principles
I'm talking about are very, very old,
Almost as old as yon foothills, as old
as the oldest monkey you can picture.

ii.

My name is Anatoly Karpov. Excuse my
beleaguered appearance. I have spent two
excruciating weeks tutoring the biggest
dumbass in the chess world, Thomas Johnston
of United States. Simply by allowing him
to watch me play I had my ears filled
with the most ridiculous stories of alligators,
field trips gone awry, advice for making tea,
advice for what kind of siding to put on my house,
and then the queerest most hollow laughter,
and in all of it I felt that I was going crazy,
even crazier than when Robert Fischer
threw his gin and tonic at me, than when
Kasparov taunted me with his ping pong paddle,
than when Kramnik kissed my girlfriend,
all put together! I am telling you, Americans,
it was the worst experience ever!

TWO CRIMINALS

Two criminals, it seems, were eating breakfast.
One ate so many breakfast he forgot to pay the waiter
And on his way out knocked over the pajama stand:
How un-cornfield in the aspect of light-to-water ratio.

As it happens, a certain police officer was passing by.
He had become so wealthy on account of a side business
(Bribery) that he didn't even pause in the camera breaker.
Which caused all the restaurant's patrons on foot the neon sign.

Even getting him in for an interview
These days is like meeting W. for coffee:
Unless you're a hotshot African ambassador
It just ain't happenin', no how, no way.

Ten years ago he named his daughter Ireland.
Fifteen years ago he fell for Kim Basinger.
Five years ago they broke up.
Thirty years ago his sister Jane was born.

Ten years from now...? In 2005 his star
Is still rising, mysteriously,
Like an Applebee's balloon over Santa Fe.
He is a confident, slightly scary man.

ERNEST BORGNINE MAD LIB

Born in [year] in [name of city] to Charles Borgnino and Anna Boselli,
[nationality] immigrants, young Ernesto first distinguished himself
as a/an [adjective] skateboarder at [last name of famous person]
Academy, causing his [plural noun] to hurl insults and throw [adjective]
cheese during the lunch hour. In [year] he was accepted to the famous
[adjective] Theater and shortly thereafter traveled to [city in California]
to star in the movie "From Here to [noun]" with [first name of person in
room] Sinatra. Sinatra turned out to be a total [noun] who drank about
ten [plural name of cocktail] a night and massaged his [body part] in the
corner until [time of morning]. Borgnine [adverb] won an Academy
Award for Best [noun] for the movie, "[first name]." During the 1960s
Borgnine was best known as the star of the televised sitcom, "McHale's
[branch of military]," and in the 1980s played a role in the television
[noun], "Airwolf." During his lifetime, Borgnine has [past tense verb] five
wives, among them Tony-award winning Ethel Merman, the [adjective]
actress whose final movie role was in the hit comedy, "Airplane," in
which [adjective] [plural noun] try to [verb] their [plural body part]
until they [verb]. For some reason, Borgnine is still alive and living in
[city name], [state name].

FOR BEN AFFLECK'S DAUGHTER

Your father is so hot. I'm serious.

The highly publicized photo of him
Wearing a Red Sox ball cap—wow.
The stubble! That bisexual grin!

He's been with Gwyneth.
Then came "Bennifer"
With a pink rock
The size of Plymouth.
Now a different Jennifer
And you, little Violet,
Cursed forever to explain
Who your famous daddy is,
What it's been like
Growing up this way,
But hey:

I would like Ben Affleck to read me bedtime stories.
I hope he takes time to read you bedtime stories.

TIM BURTON EXPLODES

Narrowly gathered zoot suit,
Extreme nose, slightly tilted,
You walked for awhile and exploded.

IN BED WITH MERYL STREEP

Hard to believe your first movie
Came out in 1977—you are timeless,
Like a Dracula statue in the rain:
And now, as you rub my shoulders,
Wearing that flowered nightgown,
We hear actual rain, or is it wind,
Rushing around our Buena Vista condo.
You click off Cheers. I know what's next.

POLANSKI'S PANOPTICON

Perspicuity of presentation, security,
Sex with a 13-year-old in 1977,
Symmetry, story: Manson shld be
The one doing time, not you—
For cracking that Krakovite mind:
Sharon Tate fertilizing flowers.
Mia Farrow picnicking in them.
Imagine this in a spinning glass stadium.

Half of the West wants you dead,
You genius, son of a plastics dealer!

MICHAEL LANDON AS A MELVILLE CHARACTER

Am I a cannon-ball, he asks,
That thou wouldst wad me
In that fashion?

And grasps the brim of his flat hat
And draws it down around his ears
And answers, resolutely, *No!*

But go thy ways; I had forgot,
He carries on, and turns to walk
Into a golden field of TV light,

Down, dog, and kennel!
I'll be home before nightfall,
Half-pint. I'll see you then.

He looks back at the camera,
Smiles, and one can see
A gorgeous sparkle in his teeth.

MY FACTOTUM

My factotum brings me tea.
Then he stands on his heels, looking
out the bay window.

Hands in pockets, a kind of
George Wallace posture.

What if none of this is real?
He muses, a little quietly.

My factotum borrows my keys
to go to the grocery store.
He brings home Rolaids
and a case of AB.

What if none of this is meaningful?
He asks, as if no time had passed.
He pours himself a cup of tea.

My factotum tries to figure out
His new digital camera.
He wants to capture the image
of a hummingbird floating
outside the bay window.

My factotum is deaf.
He wants more than he can have.

MY FACTOTUM

My factotum reneged on his promise
to take baby munchkin to the zoo
while I was fixing the Datsun.

Instead he painted pink diamonds
on my corduroys, a project he
was supposed to have finished a week ago.

MY FACTOTUM

My factotum lives in France.
My factotum has no pants.

PUSHKIN

Beautiful man looking around
with hair like iron and the eyes of a clown,
darting across the street at the first
sign of a break in the parade of carriages,
a sheaf of political poems under your arm:
I love you and miss you after all these centuries.

I am saddest, I guess, about your scandal-torn marriage
that ended with gunplay and you falling down.
I picture the single smoky burst
and can't help but wonder why you let him shoot first.
On that frozen day, had you no intention of bringing harm
to anyone at all, you gentleman—not even young d'Anthés?

EATING DINNER WITH LOUIS ZUKOFSKY

Eating dinner with Louis Zukofsky,
Watching as he examined his chops,
I rued the liquid gray restaurant light
That, playing upon dull tableware,
Drew up no perceptible sparkle,
And died away as it entered his wine.

We were young and beady-eyed
Knowing exactly how to get
That which we could no longer want,
Having been robbed of naturalness
By an endless shadow that bathed our beds,
Our legs spread out in boring forks.

That was the night of the cavalcade
That for months we had planned to attend.
He gazed at me with raccoon-ringed eyes
And said something eternal with his mouth,
Stood up and laid his napkin down
And walked off into the bathroom's shade.

Eating dinner with Louis Zukofsky,
Waiting as he perhaps relieved himself,
I rued the hundred winking lamps
Designed to provide ambience.
I read the menu once again
And wished I'd ordered Cornish hen.

FOR WALT WHITMAN

i.

I glare at a brick of grass,
stunned at its insouciance.

Why the sparkly packaging,
O pricey block of hash?

Perhaps a face more demure
would suit your gravity

mo better than sich brite
weavings under sky, my bonnet!

ii.

In this one I plan
to describe peas on stem,
bolt-upright willows, and
a harsh-lit glade
where I wake up ice-like.

There I think about you,
Walt, who celebrated himself.
I am a man of tender means,
only a bag and a bonnet,
and no money innit.

BRUCE BEASLEY!

Bruce Beasley! Your book still sits unread on my shelf
as it has since 1988! I have to admit! It was Halpern's blurb
that scared me most! "The abundance of phlegmatic
narrative"! Then there's the black and white author photo!
You look too thoughtful! And yikes, those loafers!
Then there's the fourth line of the first poem!
"A pink scab along the bottom of each bloom"!
I do not like poems that refer to pink scabs on bottoms!
Just as a general rule, mind you, Bruce Beasley!
And later in the same poem! "You can smell it on every bush"!
Smell what though! I bet you'll tell us! Ah yes!
"This hankering to get born"! That's such a weird word!
"Hankering"! I am hankering to put your book back!
I wonder if this first edition is worth anything by now!
I don't mind just leaving it on my shelf though! It's OK!

HEARTWOOD

"Not unlike a young Robert Frost"
in that you often mention trees
and weeds and that your verse
seems drenched in what one might
call rain, or in at least a poet's rain,
which strikes me as not quite the same
as other kinds of rain, Eric Pankey,
but Frost was never blurbed by Strand,
said to have spoken "with a special force,"
or commended for "his effortless command,"
nor do I recall him having gaffed
as you do in the poem "Family Matters,"
in which a drunken grandmother is said
to have fallen "onto the unmade
safety of the bed." Isn't a bed's safety
inherently "made," even if the bed itself's
"unmade," by which I take you to mean
that its linens are not straightened?
In any case, congrats for winning
the 1984 Walt Whitman Award
and then publishing *Heartwood*
a scant four years later. Bruce Beasley
published *Spirituals* in 1988, too!
Have you ever met Bruce Beasley?
Do you guys ever email each other?

HIDDEN MICROPHONES

I am all about hidden microphones.
If you pay me a certain amount of money,
I will plant a certain number of microphones
around your home, or a friend's home.

THINGS THAT TEND NOT TO COLLAPSE

My cousin Adam, the Moon, my Wedding Ring,
a Clock, a Stereo, a Book of Verse.

Try putting "Collapsing" in front of Each and see.
Suddenly the Wedding Ring collapsed.
We waited while the Stereo finished collapsing.
We saw Adam collapse on the Soccer Field.
Okay, wait, take my cousin Adam off the list.

Some things collapse only once.

A Building, an Oil Rig, a Star, a Roller Coaster.

Some things collapse many times.

A Tee-Pee, a Slinky, a Ham Sandwich, my Grandmother.

Some things absolutely never collapse.

A Stone from the shore of Lake Superior, God.

THE END OF MY COMPUTER

At the end of my computer
Sits a white hermit playing invisible chess.
He alternates between playing against me
And playing against himself for the championship.
He held the title for six straight years
But then relinquished it to himself last summer.
Whenever I go to the end of my computer
The white hermit introduces himself
As though we have never met.
Next time I am bringing a cannon
To destroy him and that tiki hut he sits in
So that I can put on my Wayfarers
And go past the end of my computer.

THE END OF MY COMPUTER

At the end of my computer
Grows a daisy that looks like a girl's basketball team.
It speaks in the manner of Alan Alda,
Very familiarly, but with multiple mouths.
I was once confined to the area
Around the end of my computer
By an invisible fence.
Prior to that, I didn't even know about it.
Nowadays I own the end of my computer.
All I ask is that the girls play hard—
They chant, *When people are laughing,*
They're generally not killing one another.
I smile as they begin to execute fundamentals.

THE BERBERS

No one knows where the Berbers came from.
These men—mostly young, with polished horns—
and their dames came chugging into Northern
Europe on their steeds from unknown origin

dragging wooden carts of goodies to trade
with the Dutch and Latvian indigenous tribes.
They cussed up a storm, which bothered our
Christian grandparents. They brought neither silks

nor tapestries but small, crudely-made books
of jokes and erotic stories, boxes of carved rocks
and bottles of the tiny black eggs. They wore
wool caps which spiraled to an odd point

and heavy coats, under which the leaders
carried prototypes of the pewter muskets
which would later turn up in English and French
fields. These bloody gadgets often backfired

or simply fell apart. A Berber woman would
hide her husband's broken gun in waterfalls, tar pits,
or drop it into a steam vent or smoking crevice,
typically. Also, after four years of quiet mating

if the woman were satisfied she would dip
her best anklet into her husband's stew
in the evening while he ate. If he were to bang
down his ladle it meant four more years.

If not, she would swallow the anklet herself,
a sign of penitence. It is from these odd rituals that
we Americans and Europeans have developed
several of our own traditions. You may wonder

which traditions I mean, and I would suggest
that you know. If you think very, very hard.

A VIOLENT VISIGOTH

As time goes by I grow to love
Angie, the sister of Visigoth 719,
more and more and more.

She wears her hair in little curls
and usually shows up in a soft black
shirt. I love to see her on the phone,

the way she cradles the cordless
between head and tender shoulder,
the way she hums tunelessly

in the shower. Her brother, though,
is a vandal, a bar-bar, the worst kind
of Visigoth. His hair is cropped

in a kind of churlish swoop and his
wingtip laces have those metal caps.
His pager is always sounding;

usually it's his agent. Angie merely
flutters her painted lids and sighs, stirs
the eggs, ever-patient. When he fires

up a cig I can tell he's an arson,
a kindler of fagots. Scorpion-like he
saunters back to his green Trans Am

and leaves Angie and me in possession
of the dooryard. Her silver pumps sparkle
and her skirt swells as she sprays the roses

with water and sprinkles Miracle Gro
on their bed. Her green eyes shine, she
takes me up in to our flannel-sheeted bed

and stirs a straw in her tea as I fall asleep.
For hours she will read a dime detective novel
while I dream off into the swirling night.

A HORSESHOE OF ROSES

Millions of years ago astrologers taught people how to fly. *They did?*
   Yes, they flew slowly at first, the traditional skirts flapping around
their thighs as they rose into a blue abyss. *What a dream!* Less than
   two decades later the gun was invented, and any historian worth a penny
will tell you that it was all downhill from there. *I've heard of this.*
   Rambling city senators, huge tracks, and statues which cost fortunes
to build and more to maintain. Moatless ranches also came into vogue
   during that time. *Lord have mercy.* But bad times will come, that much we've
learned. It's the youthful levity that predicates those times which we must
   hang like a garland around the neck of the next generation. *I'll remember
you said it.* Then they'll be safe, and with any luck they'll behave
   like the charming little monsters we dreamed of. *Whom shall I say—?*
Until 10,000 trees and clouds rise and fall into their pools, and their kids
   find them in a minty bed of chlorine, face down. They will be nicely aged.
Who has sent me? They will have long wills, long white hair hooping
   out like mops, moving at the speed of classical music into heaven's ocean.

THE MAN WITH NO HAT

Earlier that same *siècle* several prominent portraitists
had produced efforts, all commissioned by the same spinster
(though separately and under an assortment of pseudonyms),
of the fabled "Man Without a Heart," none with any
particular success, due partly to the general scarcity of knowledge
of him during that period, partly to the unwillingness of the last
of his surviving contemporaries to speak much about that
treacherous time. Known variously as Simone, Ms. Salmon,
Ms. Sullerton, Sally, as well as a number of names sounding
like Gretta or Gerta, the so-called "country spinster"
spent somewhere close to sixty thousand francs in her search
for the right likeness. But when Bradley's remarkable
Man With No Hat finally made its debut in Frankfurt—
its visage so similar in so many respects, however coincidentally,
to that of the original traitor—and after fifty or so years
of what can only be termed a fallowness in the art world—
even then there was surprisingly little interest among the fashionable
set, who by that time had turned their monocles Parisward
and therefore in the direction of (perhaps you guess correctly)
Der Dedderer, André Swingle, and the Blue Smoke Group,
which ten years previously had made its first impressions
in the salons. Now safe for general consumption,
the artwork of the Blue Smoke Group could in no way
be construed as seeking to save the by then century-old past,
but sought rather to sully it in aesthetic ash. "It must be new,"
rang the popular slogan, and served as a clarion call
(to say the least) to those of the country spinster's generation,
who at one time would have spent everything on even
the remotest possibility of resurrecting the Revolution intact.

THE WEST

Each train bound for the West
contains death in the form of anxious gunmen.
The West served as a storm drain for a time,
but the weather has not abated.
The high school at Silver Ridge was built
on the corpses of 1,500 tribesmen.

Each train bound for the West
transports people of different creeds nodding off
into metal bowls of chili topped with onions & cheese.
In their heads they think of sales calls,
but in their hearts thunder the mysterious blue oceans,
wave shapes memorized from colorized postcards.

Each train bound for the West
represents a technological watershed of sorts.
The "left coast," as it's called, has provided safe haven
for inventors for over a hundred years.
I checked my facts in a book by Louis Coe.
In fact, Berkeley has housed countless scientists.

Each train bound for the West
carries with it the scent of New Jersey honeysuckle,
a fragile stowage smelling of the Pennsylvania hills.
Western air swirls full of tumbleweed
and desert rose. Passengers are enraptured by it
as they examine the hands that've been dealt them.

Each train bound for the West
opens a historical vista. Lost pocket watches tick
in the grasses upon which they were flung. Each train carries
barrels of pickles through hollow lowlands
of lupine murmurs, complicated trees, buffalo ghosts.
I checked my facts; the weather has not abated.

OBSERVATIONS AND RECOMMENDATIONS

The porpoises are on the rise,
shedding their leathery skins.
For instance, they are beginning to mark
the graves of their leaders.
As such, they no longer respond
to our charitable donations of small shiny fish.
In conclusion, we should veer our skiffs
and tankers far to the west of that peninsula.

The junipers are falling over
as though the sun hadn't shone for days.
For instance, that one looks like a holiday tree
hung with too many crystal stars.
As such, the moon glows down on our encampment
as it did in the days when God ruled the world.
In conclusion, we will abandon candlemaking
in favor of logging and gardening for a time.

Aurora Borealis appears to be floating east,
and all our flocks are following it.
For instance, Citizen Parker's bulls
broke through a stone wall just last night.
As such, our lines of communication
and transportation have been suspended.
In conclusion, let us do research in the library
to see if this has ever happened before.

Sales of small handguns are skyrocketing
together with those of small holsters and hand grenades.
For instance, one of our trading posts
collapsed recently under the weight of fur-clad shoppers.
As such, manufacturers of other products
are experiencing unfair losses.
In conclusion, we must reinforce our buildings with steel
and possibly look into paving our streets.

SEVEN BASTIONS

The first is the bastion of hope;
it is the most popular, and scads of tourists
snap photos of their families in front of it
(that's where they post directions to the hotel).

The second is the bastion of freedom.
No one goes to it, because obviously
it is a joke.

The third is the bastion of anxiety.
A few vendors roll their carts around its grassy
yard, but they don't get much business.

The fourth is the bastion of unnecessary words.
That's where gardenias and lilies grow,
where millionaires sleep in the brush.

The fifth is the bastion of olden days,
called that because the Revolutionary Mr. Eddy
Williamson and his entourage napped in its shadow
one sultry afternoon that smelt of burnt powder.

The sixth is under construction
and will be available for viewing next spring.

The seventh, of course, is the bastion of God.
Everyone wants to visit it, but it is way up on a precipice
and is guarded by hundreds of jealous husbands
whose wives were stolen by marauders.

O SISTERS

O Sisters of the Circle of St. John and St. Festus, save us.
Sisters of the Immobilized Railway Fort, come close to us
in our time of need. Sisters of the Holy Nameless One,
we petition thee to come. Sisters of Wentzville High School,
you have scared us into being a tame group of students.
Sisters of the First Snows of May, of the Dewy Snowdrops
Drooping, come to us now, for we need you very much.
Sisters of the Sisterhood of St. Paul the Holy Man of God,
put down your bingo chits for just one moment: we need thee.
Sisters Among Serpents, and Sisters Who Sleep Sitting Up,
and Holy Sisters of the Hidden Rood, of the Crossed Staves,
and also Sisters of the Come-Hither Looks Suppressed,
come close to us now, and here, in the hour of our need,
for St. Louis, Missouri can be bleak this time of year, and cold,
and you hold the keys to the heated basketball courts
at the Holy Apostolic and Unwritten Rule of St. Josephine
Community Recreation Center, and we want to play some hoops.
Sisters of the Cardinal Resting Among Fig Branches, and also
you Sisters of the Leaf-Strewn Grotto of the North River Bend,
we know that you pray for us constantly, for we often see your eyes
burning as you look at us, and we beseech you: now is the hour
of our need. Come among us, brush your polyester garments
against us, let us touch your habits of white, of gray, of black,
O Holy Sisterhood of St. Peter the Swaggerer, of Nether Antioch,
and Sisters of Distant French Towns, behold us, how haggard
we appear, and bless us, teach us, assuage our guilt, our fear.

LIFE IS A DIRTY SECRET

Life is a dirty secret
that literature exalts.

For instance,
I am not wearing pants,

but that's not all:
I never do

when I'm alone
and thinking of you.

It's up to the poem
to set this right,

and not only that:
to make it seem grand.

2414779

Made in the USA